Heinemann First
ENCYCLOPEDIA

Volume 4
Duc-Fra

Heinemann Library
Chicago, Illinois

© 1999, 2006 Heinemann Library
a division of Reed Elsevier Inc.
Chicago, Illinois

Customer Service   888–454–2279

Visit our website at www.heinemannlibrary.com

Series Editors: Rebecca and Stephen Vickers, Gianna Williams
Author Team: Rob Alcraft, Catherine Chambers, Sabrina Crewe, Jim Drake, Fred Martin, Angela Royston, Jane Shuter, Roger Thomas, Rebecca Vickers, Stephen Vickers

This revised and expanded edition produced for Heinemann Library by Discovery Books.
Photo research by Katherine Smith and Rachel Tisdale
Designed by Keith Williams, Michelle Lisseter, and Gecko
Illustrations by Stefan Chabluk and Mark Bergin

Originated by Ambassador Litho Limited
Printed in China by WKT Company Limited

10 09 08 07 06
10 9 8 7 6 5 4 3 2

Library of Congress Cataloging-in-Publication Data

Heinemann first encyclopedia.
    p.   cm.
    Summary: A fourteen-volume encyclopedia covering animals, plants, countries, transportation, science, ancient civilizations, US states, US presidents, and world history
    ISBN 1-4034-7111-8 (v. 4 : lib. bdg.)
    1.   Children's encyclopedias and dictionaries.
I. Heinemann Library (Firm)
AG5.H45 2005
031—dc22   2005006176

Acknowledgments
Cover: Cover photographs of a desert, an electric guitar, a speedboat, an iceberg, a man on a camel, cactus flowers, and the Colosseum at night reproduced with permission of Corbis. Cover photograph of the Taj Mahal reproduced with permission of Digital Stock. Cover photograph of an x-ray of a man, and the penguins reproduced with permission of Digital Vision. Cover photographs of a giraffe, the Leaning Tower of Pisa, the Statue of Liberty, a white owl, a cactus, a butterfly, a saxophone, an astronaut, cars at night, and a circuit board reproduced with permission of Getty Images/Photodisc. Cover photograph of Raglan Castle reproduced with permission of Peter Evans; Ardea London Ltd/J.M. Labat, p. 35 bottom; Bridgeman Art Library, p. 28; Mike Brown, p. 8 top; BBC Natural History Unit/John Cancalosi, p. 46 top; George Bruce, p. 42; Alan and Sandy Carey, p. 47 bottom; J. Allan Cash Ltd, pp. 10, 24, 30 top, 32, 41; Densey Clyne, p. 19 bottom; Martin Colbeck, p. 18; Mark Deeble and Victoria Stone, pp. 13 bottom, 37 top; Adrian Dennis/AFP/Getty Images, p. 25; Gail Devers, p. 21; Empics, p. 25; FLPA/Fritz Polking, p. 33 bottom; Robert Francis, p. 16; Warren Faidley, p. 8 bottom; David Fleetham, p. 19 top; Paul Franklin, p. 45 top; Simon Fraser, p. 31; Christian Gazimek, p. 44; Jose Luis Grande, p. 5 bottom; Ronald Grant Archive/Walt Disney Co., p. 29 bottom; Sally and Richard Greenhill Photo Library/Sally Greenhill, p. 23; C.W. Helliwell, p. 20 bottom; Mike Hill, p. 37 bottom; The Hutchison Library, p. 14; Keystone/Getty Images, p. 11 top; J. Knighton, p. 7; Tom Leach, p. 5 top; Michael Leach, p. 27; Zig Leszczynski, p. 4; Renee Lynn, p. 47 top; Alistair MacEwen, p. 38; Peter Menzel, p. 17; John Mitchell, p. 9 top; MPI/Getty Images, p. 11 bottom; David Parker, p. 17 right; PhotoDisk, p. 26 bottom; Jeff Rotman, p. 34 bottom; Hans Reinhard, p. 45 bottom; Charles Tyler, p. 30 bottom; Redferns, p. 43; Tony Stone Worldwide/Ary Diesendruck, p. 39 top; Roger Sackman, p. 12; F. Schussler/PhotoLink, p. 40; Tim Shepard, p. 9 bottom; Robert A. Tyrrell, p. 13 top; Tony Stone Worldwide/Gavin Hellier, p. 15; Trip/Joseph Okwesa, p. 22; Trevor Clifford Photography, p. 48; Alan Thornton, p. 36; Sygma, p. 39; Jorg and Petra Wegner, p. 6; Mark Wilson/Getty Images, p. 26 top; Konrad Wothe, p. 20 top.

Welcome to
Heinemann First Encyclopedia

What is an encyclopedia?

An encyclopedia is an information book. It gives the most important facts about many different subjects. This encyclopedia has been written for children who are using an encyclopedia for the first time. It covers many of the subjects from school and others you may find interesting.

What is in this encyclopedia?

In this encyclopedia, each topic is called an *entry*. There is one page of information for every entry. The entries in this encyclopedia explain

- animals
- plants
- dinosaurs
- countries
- geography
- history
- world religions
- music
- art
- transportation
- science
- technology
- states
- famous Americans

How to use this encyclopedia

This encyclopedia has thirteen books called *volumes*. The first twelve volumes contain entries. The entries are all in alphabetical order. This means that Volume 1 starts with entries that begin with the letter A and Volume 12 ends with entries that begin with the letter Z. Volume 13 is the index volume. It also has other interesting information.

Here are two entries that show you what you can find on a page:

This is the letter that the entry starts with.

The "see also" line tells you where to find other related information.

Did You Know? boxes have fun or interesting bits of information.

Fact boxes give you details about the topic.

The Fact File tells you important facts and figures.

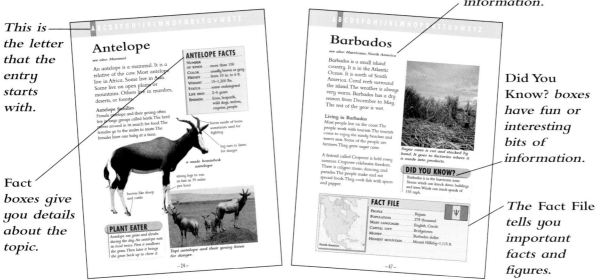

Duck

see also: Bird, Goose, Swan

A duck is a bird. It lives near water. Ducks can fly and dive. There are many kinds of wild ducks. They live all over the world. Some ducks are raised on farms. People eat duck meat. They use duck feathers in pillows and comforters.

DUCK FACTS

NUMBER OF KINDS	89
COLOR	Most ducks have dull, brownish coloring, but some are white and others are brightly colored.
LENGTH	10 to 30 inches
STATUS	common
LIFE SPAN	usually up to 10 years
ENEMIES	foxes, wolves, bears, large fish, people

PLANT, INSECT, AND MEAT EATER

Most ducks eat water weeds. They eat other plants and insects. Some sea ducks eat fish.

Duck families

A male is called a drake. A female is called a duck. The female lays from four to thirteen eggs in a nest. The babies are called ducklings. Ducklings can swim as soon as they hatch. Some ducks migrate in groups called flocks. The flocks fly to warm places for the winter.

a mallard drake

waterproof feathers to keep from getting wet while swimming

bill helps to strain or filter the water for food

webbed feet for swimming

A mallard duck and her ducklings swim very close to each other.

Eagle

see also: Bald Eagle, Bird, Hawk

The eagle is a bird. It is one of the biggest and strongest flying birds in the world. Eagles live in all but the coldest areas. Eagles are called birds of prey. They hunt and kill animals, birds, or fish for food.

Eagle families

A male eagle and a female eagle build a nest. The nest is made of sticks. It is built on a rock or in a large tree. The female lays up to three eggs at a time. The babies are called chicks. Usually only one chick grows to full size. The parents feed the chick in the nest for three months. The chick is called an eaglet when it begins to fly.

The golden eagle is found in Europe and North America. Only one chick is left in this nest.

EAGLE FACTS

NUMBER OF KINDS	more than 100
COLOR	mostly gray or brown with some white markings
LENGTH	2 to 3 feet
WEIGHT	up to 66 lbs.
WINGSPAN	up to 7 feet
STATUS	most are threatened
LIFE SPAN	around 20 years
ENEMIES	people

hooked beak for tearing meat

wide wings and spreading wingtip to fly and soar high

tail spreads to help move in the air

a tawny eagle

sharp claws called talons to kill and carry food

MEAT EATER

Eagles eat different things. Some eagles eat only fish. Most eagles eat small mammals, birds, and reptiles. An eagle can kill and eat animals as big as foxes or fish as big as salmon.

Ear

see also: Human Body, Sound

Humans and animals use ears to hear. Parts of the ear also help us to balance.

How the human ear works

The outer ear catches the sounds. It leads the sounds into the ear passage where the most important parts of the ear are protected inside the skull. The sounds hit the eardrum. The eardrum shakes. The shaking eardrum makes tiny bones inside the ear move. These tiny bones are called the hammer, anvil, and stirrup. When the tiny bones move, they make the cochlea move. The cochlea turns the movements into messages. Nerves carry the messages to the brain. The brain understands the messages.

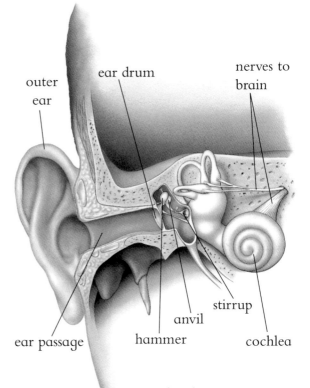

outer ear — ear drum — nerves to brain — stirrup — anvil — hammer — cochlea — ear passage

the human ear

Some animals have very special ears. Rabbits have very good hearing so that they can run away when they hear enemies.

Earth

see also: Planet, Solar System, Weather

The Earth is our planet. It is one of nine planets that move through space around the Sun. It takes one year to travel once around the Sun. The Sun keeps the Earth warm. The Earth is the right distance from the Sun to be warm enough for people, animals, and plants. If the Earth were too hot, all the water would dry up.

What makes up the Earth?

The Earth has an outer skin. It is hard rock. It is called the crust. Oceans and seas cover three-fourths of the Earth's surface. Land covers the rest of the surface. A layer of gases surrounds the Earth. This is its atmosphere. All the Earth's weather is in its atmosphere.

Inside the Earth

The Earth is very hot inside the crust. It is hot enough to melt rock. Sometimes hot liquid rock comes to the surface through the opening of a volcano.

DID YOU KNOW?

The deepest hole ever drilled into the Earth was more than seven miles. This was in Russia in 1989.

The Earth is a beautiful, blue planet. This is what North and South America look like from space.

EARTH FACTS

DISTANCE AROUND
THE EQUATOR . . . . 24,886 miles

DISTANCE FROM THE
SURFACE TO THE CENTER . . 3,912 miles

TEMPERATURE IN
THE EARTH'S CORE . . . . 8,100°F

DISTANCE OF THE
EARTH FROM THE SUN . . . . . 93 million miles

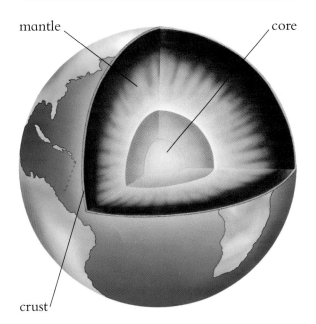

mantle core

crust

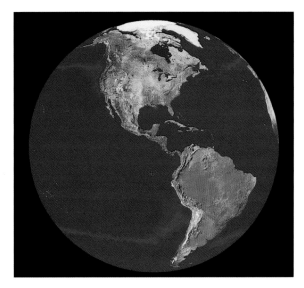

Earthquake

see also: California, Earth

An earthquake is when the ground shakes violently. An earthquake can split the land with giant cracks. It can shake apart buildings. It can cause giant tidal waves in the oceans. Most earthquakes happen along cracks in the earth's surface.

Why are there earthquakes?

Earthquakes happen when the rocks inside the earth's crust move. The movement spreads like ripples in a pond. These are called shock waves. The shock waves make the ground shake.

People and earthquakes

Scientists can measure the movement of rocks inside the earth. Sometimes scientists can predict where and when an earthquake will happen. Sometimes there is no warning at all. Some parts of the world have more earthquakes than other parts. Most earthquakes are too small to be felt, but every year, a few earthquakes cause damage and death.

Scientists measure what is happening in the earth's crust using an instrument like this one.

DID YOU KNOW?

The shaking at the site of an earthquake lasts from a few seconds to a few minutes.

This is some of the damage done by an earthquake in California in 1994. Many buildings and roads were destroyed.

Earwig

see also: Insect

An earwig is an insect. It has two large pincers at the tail end of its body. Earwigs live under stones and in fallen trees. They live all over the world, but mostly in hot countries. Earwigs have wings, but they seldom fly.

EARWIG FACTS

NUMBER OF KINDS	about 1,000
COLOR	brown
LENGTH	up to 2 inches
STATUS	common
ENEMIES	birds, small mammals

long antennae to touch, smell, and feel

thin back wings fold under the hard front wings

pincers to hold food and nip enemies

hard, shiny covering to protect the body

a male earwig

Earwig families

A female earwig digs a small hole. She lays eggs in the hole. She stays with the eggs until they hatch. Young earwigs are called nymphs. The female earwig stays with the nymphs until they can care for themselves.

PLANT, INSECT, AND MEAT EATER

Earwigs feed at night. They help in the garden by eating snails and caterpillars. They can do harm in the garden, too. They damage flowers and fruit as they eat.

These hatching nymphs look like adults, but they have no wings.

Ecuador

see also: Incas, South America

Ecuador is a country in South America. The high Andes Mountains run through the center of the country. To the east of the mountains are hot, rainy forests. To the west of the mountains are swamps, deserts, and good farm land.

DID YOU KNOW?

The Galapagos Islands are part of Ecuador. The islands have unusual animals.

Living in Ecuador

Half of Ecuador's people live along the coast. Many people work in Guayaquil, a large port city. Families who live in the mountains have small farms. They keep llamas. Llamas are woolly animals with long necks. Llamas are used for wool and meat. They are used to carry loads, too.

The Quéchua Native Americans were some of Ecuador's first people. They still live in the Andes Mountains. The women wear long colorful skirts. Each village has its own style of hat. The men wear loose coats called ponchos.

Many of the native people of Ecuador still wear their traditional clothes. This family has dressed in their best clothes to go to church.

South America

FACT FILE

PEOPLE	Ecuadorians
POPULATION	about 13 million
MAIN LANGUAGES	Spanish, Quéchua
CAPITAL CITY	Quito
BIGGEST CITY	Guayaquil
MONEY	Sucre
HIGHEST MOUNTAIN	Chimborazo—20,565 feet
LONGEST RIVER	Guayas River—100 miles

Edison, Thomas

see also: Electricity

Thomas Edison was an inventor. He invented the light bulb and many other inventions that used electricity.

Edison goes to work

Edison was born in Milan, Ohio, on February 11, 1847. He only went to school for three months. The rest of the time, his mother taught him at home.

Edison started selling candy and newspapers on trains when he was twelve. Then Edison became a telegraph operator. The telegraph sent messages along wires.

DID YOU KNOW?

Edison invented a movie camera called a kinetograph. He also made a kinetoscope, which could show short movies.

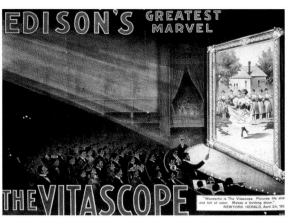

This ad is publicizing the Vitascope, an early form of movie projector.

Edison's laboratory was in Orange, New Jersey.

KEY DATES

1847 .. Thomas Edison is born.
1877 .. Edison invents the microphone and phonograph.
1879 .. Edison invents a usable electric light bulb.
1889 .. Edison invents a movie camera.
1931 .. Edison dies.

Edison's great inventions

Edison's first inventions were to do with the telegraph and similar machines. His microphone made it possible for people to use telephones. His phonograph was the first device for recording and playing music.

Before Edison, people used candles, oil lamps, or gaslights to light rooms. Edison invented a light bulb and a system for electric light. In 1882, the first electrical power plant opened in New York. Edison's inventions led the way to many other great inventions.

Eel

see also: Fish, Sea Life

An eel is a long, thin fish. It looks like a snake. Most eels live in shallow seawater. Some eels live at the bottom of the deepest seas. Some eels live in fresh water.

EEL FACTS

NUMBER OF KINDS	about 600
COLOR	silver and black
LENGTH	up to 10 feet
STATUS	common
LIFE SPAN	about 11 years
ENEMIES	other fish, squid, people

Eel families

An eel begins life as an egg. A young eel is called an elver. Some elvers float great distances. They float from the Caribbean Sea to the coasts of Europe or North America. They grow and change color for ten years until they are adult eels. Then some of the eels return to the Caribbean to lay eggs.

long fin along the back and tail to keep the eel from rolling over

wiggling tail and body to move through water

gills for breathing underwater

an eel

fins for steering

PLANT AND MEAT EATER

Eels eat plankton, fish, and animals that live on the ocean floor. Many deep-sea eels have huge mouths for catching large fish.

These young elvers are hiding in an undersea plant.

Egg

see also: Bird

An egg is the female cell of an animal or plant. An egg that has been fertilized by a male grows into a new plant or animal.

EGG FACTS

- An ostrich egg weighs up to 4 lbs.
- Cod fish can lay more than one million eggs at once.
- Sea turtles swim thousands of miles to lay their eggs on the same beach where they were born.

Different kinds of eggs

Bird eggs Female birds usually lay eggs in nests. One parent bird sits on the eggs to keep them warm. A bird's egg has a hard shell. The undeveloped bird inside the shell is called an embryo. The eggshell keeps the growing embryo safe. Most of the embryo's food is in the egg yolk. The embryo uses up the food in the yolk. The embryo grows into a baby bird. The baby bird cracks the shell. It hatches from the egg.

Reptile and amphibian eggs A female reptile usually buries her eggs. Most reptile eggs have soft shells. Amphibian females lay eggs in water. These eggs don't have shells. They are laid in a jellylike substance.

Mammal eggs Mammals also have eggs. The eggs develop inside the mother. Mammal eggs do not have yolks to feed the growing embryo. The embryo gets its food from the mother's body.

A hummingbird egg looks very tiny when it is compared to a chicken egg.

Baby crocodiles, called hatchlings, break their way out of their shells.

Egypt

see also: Africa; Egypt, Ancient; Pyramid

Egypt is a country in northeast Africa. Most of the country is desert. The land around the Nile River is not desert. There are some mountains in the northeast. There is a hot season and a cool season.

The pyramids are the burial grounds of Egypt's ancient kings.

Living in Egypt

Cairo, Egypt, is the largest city in Africa. Most Egyptians live in the Nile Valley. The Nile River floods the land along the river. This makes the soil good for growing crops. Farmers grow date palms, cotton, rice, beans, and fruit. Egyptians eat a bean paste called *ful*.

Sheep are raised and cotton is grown along the Nile River. Some of Egypt's many factories make clothes. The clothes are made from Egypt's wool and cotton.

Many tourists visit Egypt to see the statues and pyramids from Egypt's ancient past.

DID YOU KNOW?

The Suez Canal is almost 100 miles long. The canal connects the Mediterranean Sea and the Red Sea. Ships use the canal so that they do not have to travel all the way around the southern tip of Africa.

FACT FILE

Africa

PEOPLE	Egyptians
POPULATION	about 76 million
MAIN LANGUAGES	Arabic, English, French
CAPITAL CITY	Cairo
MONEY	Egyptian pound
HIGHEST MOUNTAIN	Jabal Katherina—8,655 feet
LONGEST RIVER	Nile River—4,145 miles

Egypt, Ancient

see also: Egypt, Hieroglyphics, Pyramid

The ancient Egyptians lived in Egypt from 3000 B.C. to 30 B.C. They lived in the Nile Valley. The valley flooded each year leaving behind mud that became good soil for growing crops. The rest of Egypt was desert. Egypt became part of the Roman Empire when the Romans took over in 30 B.C.

What were the ancient Egyptians like?

Ancient Egypt was very organized. It had a ruler called a pharaoh. The pharaoh was in charge of Egypt and its religion. Government officials were priests. Most of the people were farmers.

The ancient Egyptians believed in many gods and goddesses. They believed that unhappy gods and goddesses could bring trouble to Egypt. The people tried to keep the gods and goddesses happy. They prayed to the gods and goddesses. They gave them presents.

For what are they known?

The ancient Egyptians are known for building pyramids and the tombs in the Valley of the Kings. As part of their burial practices, they preserved the bodies of the dead. The ancient Egyptians are also known for their picture writing called hieroglyphics.

KEY DATES

3000 B.C.	The first pharaoh, King Menes, rules Upper and Lower Egypt
2686 B.C.–2160 B.C.	The first pyramid is built around 2650 at Saqqara. The "Old Kingdom" went from 2686-2181 B.C.
2133 B.C.–1786 B.C.	The capital is moved to Thebes.
1567 B.C.–1085 B.C.	Many great pharaohs rule: Hatshepsut, the woman pharaoh, and Ramses II.
1085 B.C.–1030 B.C.	Temple of Khons is completed.
30 B.C.	Romans take over.

Much of what we know about everyday life in ancient Egypt comes from studying the painted walls of tombs.

El Salvador

see also: North America

El Salvador is a small country in Central America. It has mountains and volcanoes. The climate there is cool. The coast in the west is along the Pacific Ocean. The climate there is warm and wet.

Living in El Salvador

People travel across the city of San Salvador in brightly-painted buses. San Salvador has a parade twice a year. The parade is called Festival of the Savior. People carry an ancient religious statue in the parade.

More than half of the people live in the country. Families have small farms. They grow corn and coffee. People eat rice or beans with most meals. They also eat tortillas.

DID YOU KNOW?

El Salvador's environment is damaged. It once had dense forests. Now, the forests have almost disappeared.

This fruit seller is pulling his handcart through a busy street.

North America

FACT FILE

PEOPLE	El Salvadorans
POPULATION	about 6 million
MAIN LANGUAGE	Spanish
CAPITAL CITY	San Salvador
MONEY	Colón, U.S. Dollar
HIGHEST MOUNTAIN	Cerro El Pital–7,933 feet
LONGEST RIVER	Lempa River–199 miles

Electricity

see also: Energy, Heat, Light

Electricity is energy. It makes things work. It makes motors, heaters, and TVs work. Electricity moves along wires. It can also be stored and carried in batteries.

How is electricity made?

Electricity is made in power stations. Some power stations use gas or coal to make electricity. Other power stations turn water, solar, nuclear, or wind power into electricity. Power lines carry electricity to homes, schools, offices, and factories.

People and electricity

Electricity is clean. It is easy to use. People turn it on with a switch or a button. Anything that plugs in or runs on batteries is using electricity.

ELECTRICITY FIRSTS

1752	Benjamin Franklin experimented with a kite to prove that lightning was electricity
1800	first batteries made
1830s	generators and electric motors invented
1870s.....	electric light bulbs invented independently by both Thomas Edison and Joseph Swan
1880s	first power stations set up to provide lights in cities. The first was in 1882.

STAY SAFE

Never play with plugs or wires! Never go near power lines or transformers! Electricity can burn or kill people.

Fields of windmills collect wind energy and turn it into electricity. This wind farm is in California.

Hoover Dam, on the Arizona and Nevada border, uses the energy of flowing water to make electricity.

Elephant

see also: Mammal

The elephant is a mammal. It is the biggest and strongest animal on land. There are two kinds of elephants. They are the Asian elephant and the African elephant.

ELEPHANT FACTS

NUMBER OF KINDS	2
COLOR	gray–brown
LENGTH	16 to 20 feet
HEIGHT	9 to 11 feet
WEIGHT	up to 13 thousand lbs.
STATUS	Asian elephants are endangered
LIFE SPAN	up to 70 years
ENEMIES	People kill elephants for their tusks.

big ears flap for keeping cool

trunk to drink, bathe, smell, breathe, and lift things

tusks for fighting and digging for water

tail to swish away insects

an African elephant

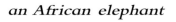

PLANT EATER

An elephant can eat 440 pounds of grass and leaves every day and drink more than 25 gallons of water at a time.

Elephant families

A male is called a bull. A female is called a cow. A cow has one baby at a time. The baby is called a calf. Cows and calves live together in groups called herds. Bull elephants live by themselves.

This African elephant cow is with her young calf and a new baby.

Emu

see also: Australia, Bird

The emu is a large bird. It does not fly. It can run as fast as 25 miles per hour. The emu is found on the grasslands of Australia.

Emu families

The male emu builds a nest on the ground. As many as three female emus might lay their eggs in one nest. The male sits on the eggs until the chicks hatch from the eggs. He feeds them and guards them for about five months. When the chicks are grown, the emus move around in small groups. The emus wander looking for food.

short, stubby wings that lift up to cool off in hot weather

EMU FACTS

NUMBER OF KINDS	1
COLOR	gray-brown
HEIGHT	up to 6 feet
WEIGHT	up to 110 lbs.
STATUS	common
LIFE SPAN	5 to 10 years
ENEMIES	farmers shoot emus that feed on crops

an emu

grayish-brown color helps it hide

long, strong legs to run fast

PLANT, INSECT, AND MEAT EATER

An emu likes to eat seeds, fruit, and insects. It also catches small lizards and rodents. An emu also eats large pebbles to help grind the food in its stomach.

It takes about eight weeks for emu eggs to hatch.

Pendleton Community Library

Endangered Species

see also: Animal, Plant

An endangered species is a kind of plant or animal that may become extinct. Extinct means that none of that kind of plant or animal is left alive anywhere in the world. Some endangered animals live only in zoos or national parks.

Causes of extinction

One way plants and animals become extinct is when they live only in one place. If the place where they live is destroyed, the plants and animals have nowhere else to live. Then they die out.

Plants and animals can become endangered when people collect or hunt them until there are almost none left.

Laws protect some endangered plants and animals. This means that people may not collect or hunt them.

The pitcher plant grows in swamps. It is endangered because the swamps are being drained. People want to use the land where the pitcher plant lives.

STATUS OF PLANTS AND ANIMALS

How many there are of each plant and animal tells its status. The following list explains the status words used in this encyclopedia.

COMMON.........there are many of them

RARE ....not often found in the wild

THREATENED .....fewer than rare, but not yet endangered

ENDANGERED......so few that they might become extinct

Hunters kill rhinoceroses to get their horns. The rhinoceros has the status of endangered animal.

Energy

see also: Electricity, Heat, Light, Sound

Energy gives people and things the power to do work. Everything we do uses energy. Energy comes in many forms. Human beings and animals get energy from food. Electricity, light, sound, movement, and heat are other types of energy.

How energy changes

Millions of years ago trees used energy from the sun. When the trees died, they fell down. Over time the trees turned into coal. Now, power stations can use coal to make electrical energy. This electrical energy turns into heat, light, and sound energy.

Bodies store energy

An athlete has the energy to run. The athlete's body stores energy before a race. The athlete uses the energy to run the race.

This athlete has the energy to run very fast.

DID YOU KNOW?

There are many ways to save energy. Insulation in houses saves heat energy. Low-energy light bulbs use less electrical energy than regular light bulbs. Riding in a carpool saves fuel energy.

Engine

see also: Car, Electricity, Transportation

An engine is a machine. It uses energy. The energy it uses can be from a fuel. Gasoline, oil, or natural gas are fuels used by engines. Electricity can power engines, too.

ENGINE FIRSTS

100	first steam-powered toys
1712	first useful steam engine
1884	first turbine (bladed) engine
1885	first gasoline engine
1890	first diesel-powered engine
1930	first jet engine
1957	first space rocket

How do engines work?

How an engine works depends on the kind of fuel it uses. A car engine uses gasoline. It works by internal combustion. The gasoline mixes with air. A spark inside the engine lights the gasoline and air. It burns. The hot gases from the burning fuel expand. They push parts of the engine up and down. This moves the wheels.

People and engines

Cars, buses, ships, and airplanes all have engines. Engines can cause air and water pollution. Sometimes all the fuel in the engine does not burn. Then some fuel ends up in the air or water.

Most small machines used in homes have electric engines. These engines are called motors. Vacuum cleaners, washing machines, and refrigerators have motors.

This is a gasoline engine in a car.

England

see also: Northern Ireland, Scotland, United Kingdom, Wales

England is a country in Europe. It is the southern part of the island of Great Britain. England is part of the United Kingdom. Most of England is low, flat land or low hills. The highest mountains are in the northwest. There are four seasons. It rains all year round.

Living in England

Most people live in the southeast and in the city of London. The cities have office buildings and factories. Farmers grow crops. They raise cattle. People enjoy visiting castles and historic houses. They take walks in the country. Soccer, rugby, and cricket are popular sports.

DID YOU KNOW?

Cheddar cheese was first made in the village of Cheddar. Cheddar is in southwest England.

Police officers are sometimes called "bobbies." The police force was started by Sir Robert (Bobby) Peel.

Europe

FACT FILE

PEOPLE	English
POPULATION	almost 50 million
MAIN LANGUAGE	English
CAPITAL CITY	London
MONEY	Pound sterling
HIGHEST MOUNTAIN	Scafell Pike—3,210 feet
LONGEST RIVER	The Severn—220 miles

Ethiopia

see also: Africa

Ethiopia is in northeast Africa. There are mountains. There are high, flat rural areas. There are dry lowlands and desert. Ethiopia has two rainy seasons every year. One rainy season is long and the other is short.

Living in Ethiopia

Most Ethiopians live in villages in the high, central part of Ethiopia. The village houses are round with thatched roofs.

The people who live in the country grow coffee, cotton, grain, beans, and oil seeds. The biggest crop is coffee. Ethiopia sells coffee to other countries. Coffee is important to Ethiopians. They have special customs about making and serving coffee.

This woman is from Gondar Province in Ethiopia. She is serving coffee in a special, traditional way.

DID YOU KNOW?

Ethiopia had a drought in the 1980s. The lack of rain caused a food shortage. People around the world gave money to help the Ethiopians.

Africa

FACT FILE

PEOPLE	Ethiopians
POPULATION	about 68 million
MAIN LANGUAGES	Amharic, English, Arabic
CAPITAL CITY	Addis Ababa
MONEY	Birr
HIGHEST MOUNTAIN	Ras Dashan–15,163 feet
LONGEST RIVER	Abbai River–850 miles

Europe

see also: Continent

Europe is one of the seven continents. The Ural Mountains are in the east. They divide Europe from Asia. The Mediterranean Sea is between Europe and Africa. The Atlantic Ocean is to the west.

The land

The Alps are the highest mountains in Europe. There are other, smaller mountain ranges. The North European Plain is in the center. It is a big area of low land.

Climate, plants, and animals

The climate in the west is wet and cool. The south is warmer and drier. Northern Europe has very cold winters. Most of the land in Europe is used for farming. Some areas are forest. Wild animals, such as deer, mountain goats, and wolves live in the forests.

People and countries

About 730 million people live in Europe. There are 46 countries. Each country has its own language and customs. Some countries belong to the European Union. The countries of the union work together to make the countries strong and rich.

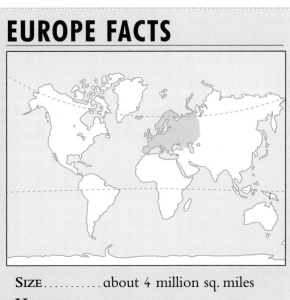

EUROPE FACTS

SIZE	about 4 million sq. miles
HIGHEST MOUNTAIN	Mount Elbrus–18,488 feet
LONGEST RIVER	Volga River–2,298 miles
SPECIAL FEATURE	The Caspian Sea is the world's biggest lake.

Soccer is very popular in Europe. This is the closing ceremony of the Euro 2004 championship, which was held in Portugal.

Executive Branch

see also: Constitution, Government, Judicial Branch, Legislative Branch

The executive branch is one of the three parts of the United States government. The Constitution says the job of the executive branch is to make sure the nation's laws are kept.

The president

The president is head of the executive branch. He or she is called the chief executive. The president has to sign laws made by the legislative branch, or Congress. The president is also commander-in-chief of the U.S. armed forces. The president represents the United States abroad and makes treaties with other nations. The president is elected every four years.

The vice president is present at this joint session of Congress held in 2005.

DID YOU KNOW?

If a president dies, the vice president takes over. The vice president is also head of the Senate. The Senate is part of the government's legislative branch.

The White House is the president's office and home in Washington, D.C.

Departments and the Cabinet

The executive branch has fifteen government departments to run. These include the Treasury, the Department of Agriculture, and the Department of Transportation. Each department except the Department of Justice has a head called a secretary. The head of the Department of Justice is called the Attorney General. All the department heads and the vice president regularly meet with the president. This group is called the Cabinet. The Cabinet helps the president make decisions. The president can choose other officials to be in the Cabinet, too.

Eye

see also: Animal, Human Body

Eyes are the parts of the body through which humans and animals see. Light bounces off objects. The light makes an image of an object. Eyes catch the light to see the image. Most parts of the human eye are kept safe inside the head.

Eye problems

When the lens of the eye is the wrong shape, the eye cannot focus. Glasses and contact lenses help eyes to focus.

DID YOU KNOW?

Animals that hunt at night have special pupils in their eyes. The pupils open very wide. This lets in as much light as possible.

The owl has big pupils. Big pupils help the owl to see in the dark.

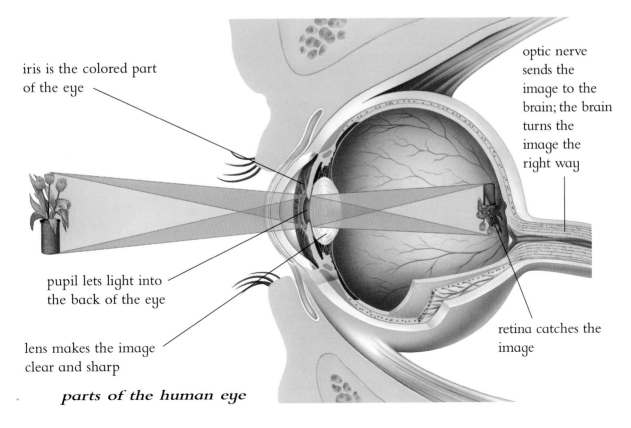

iris is the colored part of the eye

optic nerve sends the image to the brain; the brain turns the image the right way

pupil lets light into the back of the eye

lens makes the image clear and sharp

retina catches the image

parts of the human eye

Fable

see also: Legend, Literature, Myth, Story

A fable is a short story. It teaches a lesson. The lesson is called a moral. The characters in a fable are usually animals. The animals behave and talk like people.

Who wrote fables?

The most well-known fable storytellers and writers are Aesop, Jean de la Fontaine, and Gotthold Ephraim Lessing. Aesop lived in ancient Greece about 2,500 years ago. He probably was a slave on the island of Samos. Fontaine lived in France in the 1800s. Lessing lived in Germany about 100 years after Fontaine. Their stories are translated into many languages.

This illustration was made more than 200 years ago. It is for the fable "The Fox and the Grapes."

DID YOU KNOW?

In one of Aesop's fables, the fox finds an actor's mask. The mask has holes for the eyes and mouth. "Ah!" says the fox to the mask, "You are beautiful on the outside, but behind your face there is nothing!" The moral is that people should not worry about how they look. They should think about the way they behave.

BIDPAI

A wise man named Bidpai wrote a collection of animal fables. He lived in India about 1,500 years ago. Bidpai used fables to tell how a young prince should lead his life.

Fairy Tale

see also: Fable, Literature, Myth, Story

Fairy tales are children's stories. The stories have been told for hundreds of years. Not all fairy tales are about fairies. Usually they are about magic or imaginary creatures. Some fairy tales are about times long ago. Some fairy tales are about present times.

Who wrote fairy tales?

Some of the most well-known fairy tales are from the Grimm brothers. They published a book of fairy tales in the 1800s. Hans Christian Andersen lived in Denmark in the 1800s. He wrote 150 fairy tales. He wrote "Thumbelina," a story about a tiny girl.

Hans Christian Andersen wrote many well-known stories. He wrote "The Princess and the Pea" and "The Ugly Duckling."

The Grimm brothers' fairy tale "Snow White" was made into an animated movie.

JACOB GRIMM (1785–1863)

WILHELM GRIMM (1786–1859)

The Grimm brothers collected old fairy tales. The tales were hundreds of years old. They wrote the stories in a book called *Tales from the Brothers Grimm*. Two of these stories are "Hansel and Gretel" and "Snow White."

Farming

see also: Crop, Soil, Weather

Farming is the work people do to grow crops and provide food. In some places, farmers and their families eat most of what they grow. In other places, farmers grow crops to sell to other people.

Types of farming

Farmers grow grain, fruit, and vegetables to eat. They also grow cotton, tobacco, or flowers. These crops are used to make things. Farmers also raise animals.

Fields in Nepal are flooded with water. Then rice plants are planted by hand.

People and farming

People have farmed for more than nine thousand years. Some farm work is done by hand. Pitchforks, hoes, and spades are hand tools. Machinery also does farm work. Tractors pull plows. Balers bundle hay.

Some farmers use chemicals. Fertilizers help the crops grow. Insecticides and pesticides control or kill weeds and insects. Some farming is organic farming. Organic farms do not use chemicals.

Big machinery like this combine help farmers harvest huge crops.

DID YOU KNOW?

More people in the world do farming work than any other kind of work.

Fern

see also: Plant

A fern is a green plant. It does not have flowers. Ferns grow in most parts of the world. They grow best in damp, shady places. They do not grow in deserts.

Life of a fern

Ferns produce spores. They do not produce seeds. The wind blows the spores around. A spore falls to the ground. It grows into a small leaf. It is shaped like a heart. The leaf has male and female seeds. A new fern grows when a male seed and a female seed are joined.

Ferns were one of the first plants to grow on land. Millions of years ago, giant tree ferns covered much of the land. Today people grow ferns in their gardens. Ferns are also house plants.

FERN FACTS

NUMBER OF KINDS	about 10 thousand
HEIGHT	1 inch to 82 feet
LIFE SPAN	up to 100 years
ENEMIES	animals that eat ferns

Tree ferns are the largest ferns. They grow in hot, tropical countries. Tree ferns are one of the oldest types of plants still alive.

a frond of a lady fern

The leaf of a fern is called a frond. It has many smaller leaves with leaflets. Spores are found on the underside of the leaflets.

Finland

see also: Arctic, Europe

Finland is a country in northern Europe. The land is mostly low and flat. It has some hills and mountains in the north. There are many lakes and forests. Summers are warm. Winters are very cold and snowy.

Living in Finland
Most Finns live in cities in the south. People in the country live in traditional houses made of wood. Finns eat potatoes with meat or fish. The fish is often herring.

Farmers grow grain and root crops. Reindeer are raised for meat. Fish are caught and processed around the coast. Many people work in factories. The factories make paper and other things from wood.

The *kantele* is a stringed instrument played in Finland. Poetry is read as it is played.

Laplanders handle boats well. These people are wearing traditional clothing.

DID YOU KNOW?

Lapland is in the north of Finland. The people of Lapland herd reindeer and catch fish.

Europe

FACT FILE

PEOPLE	Finnish, Finns
POPULATION	about 5 million
MAIN LANGUAGES	Finnish, Swedish
CAPITAL CITY	Helsinki
MONEY	Euro
HIGHEST MOUNTAIN	Haltiatunturi—4,345 feet
LONGEST RIVER	Kemijoki River—340 miles

Firefly

see also: Beetle, Insect

A firefly is an insect. Fireflies are beetles that give off a glowing or flashing light. Fireflies are often called lightning bugs. They live all over the world. They do not live in Antarctica.

FIREFLY FACTS

NUMBER OF KINDS	1,900
COLOR	brown or black with red, yellow, or orange markings
LENGTH	less than an inch
STATUS	common
LIFE SPAN	up to 2 years
ENEMIES	birds, lizards, frogs, spiders

Firefly families

The female lays eggs in damp soil. The eggs hatch into glowworms. Each glowworm eats and grows for about two years. Then it changes into a pupa. Finally it changes into a firefly. An adult firefly lives from a few days to a month.

the underside of a Jamaican firefly

soft, but tough skin to protect the body

yellowy-green light to attract a mate; each kind of firefly has its own light

hard wing case to cover and to protect the wings

Fireflies fly in the early evening. The fireflies were moving when this photograph was taken. Their lights look like streaks in the photograph.

PLANT AND INSECT EATER

A glowworm eats flowers, snails, earthworms, and caterpillars. It kills its food with its poison. Some adult fireflies do not eat at all. Others feed on nectar. Nectar is a sweet juice made by some flowers.

Fish

see also: Fish, Tropical; Sea Life

A fish is an animal with fins, gills, and a backbone. Many fish have sharp teeth. Fish live wherever there is water. They live almost everywhere in the world. Many fish live in seas and oceans. Other fish live in ponds, lakes, rivers, and streams.

FISH FACTS

NUMBER OF KINDS	more than 20 thousand
COLOR	all colors and patterns
LENGTH	half inch to 39 feet
WEIGHT	up to 17 tons
STATUS	common
LIFE SPAN	up to 50 years
ENEMIES	other fish, squid, people

Fish families

A female fish lays her eggs in the water. The eggs hatch. Then the young fish eat the egg yolk until they can find their own food. Most young fish are called fry.

back and anal fins to keep from rolling over

gills to take in oxygen from water

tail and tail fin that move from side to side and push the fish through water

hard scales to protect the body

fins to steer through water

a cod

Some fish live on their own. Other fish swim in big groups called schools.

PLANT, INSECT, AND MEAT EATER

Most fish eat other fish and sea animals. Many fish have sharp teeth. Some fish feed on water plants. Fish also eat tiny plants and animals called plankton.

Fish, Tropical

see also: Coral, Fish, Sea Life

Tropical fish are small, colorful fish. They live in warm waters off the coasts of Australia, South America, Africa, and southern Asia. Many people keep tropical fish as pets.

Tank life

Pet fish live in water tanks called aquariums. Only fish that like the same kind of water can live together in the same tank. Most tropical fish like warm water. Some tropical fish like cooler water. Some tropical fish can only live in salt water. Some tropical fish are very fierce. Piranhas are so fierce that they have to be kept away from other fish.

Aquarium fish eat dried fish food. The tank must be kept clean. The tank must be big enough for the fish.

Tropical fish are found in the wild. These fish live near a coral reef.

plants and stones give fish places to hide

small heater keeps the water at the correct temperature

air bubbles give fish oxygen to breathe

an aquarium for tropical fish

Flag

see also: American Flag,
Communication

A flag is a piece of cloth. It has colored patterns, shapes, or symbols on it. Flags are flown from ropes, poles, or sticks. Flags may hang down from buildings. People have used flags for more than a thousand years. Flags are a way of saying something without using words.

FLAG FIRSTS

1777	American flag is first used—the number of stars changed over time
1801	modern British flag, the Union Jack, is first used
1857	flags are first used for international ship signaling
1863	Red Cross flag is first used
1901	modern Australian flag is first used
1914	Olympic flag with five linking circles is first used
1948	United Nations flag is first used

The sailor uses two flags to send a message. The positions of the flags stand for the letters of the alphabet. This flag alphabet is called semaphore.

Using flags

Countries, groups, clubs, and teams have flags. Flags say, "This is ours." Flags say, "This is who we stand for."

Armies used to carry flags into battle. An army won when it captured its opponent's flag.

Ships use special flags to signal to each other. Flags give messages even when the ship's crew does not speak the same language.

A ship that is in trouble will hang its flag upside down. This lets others know that the ship is in trouble.

Flags in motor racing signal "start," "finish," and "danger on the roadway." Everyone in the race understands the flag signals.

Flamingo

see also: Bird

A flamingo is a tall, pink bird. It lives in shallow, salty lakes. All flamingos live in warm countries.

Flamingo families

Flamingos live in a huge group called a flock. There can be thousands of flamingos in the flock. Each pair of male and female flamingos builds a mud nest in shallow water. The female lays one egg. A baby flamingo, called a chick, hatches from the egg. Both parent birds take care of the chick until it is big enough to care for itself.

PLANT, INSECT, AND MEAT EATER

Flamingos eat insect larvae, small crabs, and shrimps. The pink shrimps give flamingos their pink color.

FLAMINGO FACTS

NUMBER OF KINDS	5
COLOR	pink or pinkish-gray
HEIGHT	up to 5 feet
LENGTH	up to 65 inches
WEIGHT	4–9 lbs.
STATUS	common
LIFE SPAN	about 10 years
ENEMIES	eagles, people

beak strains food from water

long neck to reach down into the water for food

long wings to help bird fly

long legs to wade through water and mud

a lesser flamingo

A female lesser flamingo cares for her chick.

Flea

see also: Insect

A flea is an insect. It lives on warm bodies of birds and mammals. It lives everywhere in the world. Fleas are pests. They suck blood from people and animals. They carry diseases.

FLEA FACTS

NUMBER OF KINDS	1,800
COLOR	black or brown
LENGTH	much less than one inch
STATUS	common
LIFE SPAN	nearly 2 years
ENEMIES	special chemicals called insecticides

Flea families

Adult fleas lay eggs in clothing. They lay eggs in animal nests and bedding. A young flea hatches into a larva. Then three weeks to eight months later the larva spins a cocoon. It is an adult when it comes out of the cocoon. The new adult flea quickly finds a mammal or bird on which to live.

MEAT EATER

An adult flea sucks the blood of the animal on which it lives. Flea larvae feed on fallen hair, food scraps and dirt.

hard body shell to protect the flea from the scratching animal

a cat flea

hard beak to pierce an animal's skin to suck its blood

spikes on legs to move quickly through fur and feathers

long, strong back legs to jump more than twelve inches from one animal to another

This cat flea larva is feeding on blood.

Flood

see also: Delta, River, Weather

A flood is when water flows over the land. Floods can ruin crops. Floods can damage buildings. Floods can wash away people and animals.

Types of flood

Sometimes extra water from melting snow or rain runs into rivers and streams. Then the rivers and streams overflow. Some of the flood water sinks into the soil. The rest of the flood water flows back into the river or dries up in the sun.

Seawater can also flood the land. Strong winds can cause big waves to come ashore and flood the land.

The Thames Barrier in London, England, protects the city from flood water.

Many rivers overflowed their banks during the 1993 floods in the Midwest United States.

People and floods

People have always lived near rivers. They use the rivers for transportation, fishing, and washing. The land along a river is good for farming, but rivers can flood the land. There are different ways to protect people from floods. Dams across rivers can hold back extra water. River banks and sea walls can be made higher and stronger. Special diggers called dredgers can make rivers deeper so that they hold more water.

Florida

see also: United States of America

Florida is a state in the southern United States of America. Florida is nearly surrounded by water. It is on a peninsula between the Gulf of Mexico and the Atlantic Ocean. The land is mostly flat. Hurricanes can strike Florida in summer and fall.

Miami's seafront has featured in many movies.

Life in Florida

Farming and fishing are very important in Florida. Farmers grow fruit, especially oranges and grapefruit. Fishing boats bring in lobster, shrimp, and many kinds of fish.

The population of Florida is growing very fast. Older Americans like to retire there because it is warm. Other people come to Florida from Caribbean countries, especially Cuba.

DID YOU KNOW?

More kinds of fish live in Florida's lakes, rivers, and coastal waters than anywhere else in the world. Alligators live in the wetlands called the Everglades.

Lots of people in Florida work in tourism. Many tourists visit Florida every year. Tourists like to visit Disney World in Orlando and the Kennedy Space Center at Cape Canaveral.

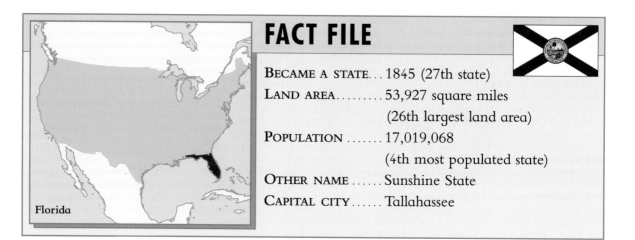

Florida

FACT FILE

BECAME A STATE	1845 (27th state)
LAND AREA	53,927 square miles (26th largest land area)
POPULATION	17,019,068 (4th most populated state)
OTHER NAME	Sunshine State
CAPITAL CITY	Tallahassee

Flower

see also: Leaf, Plant, Root, Seed, Stem

A flower is the part of a plant that produces seeds. Many flowers have brightly colored petals. Flowering plants grow almost everywhere on land. They do not grow in very cold places.

Life of a flower

The job of a flower is to make new plants. A flower can have male pollen, or it can have female ovules. One flower might have both. A grain of pollen from one flower joins with an ovule in another flower. This makes a seed. The seed might grow into a new plant.

Many people grow flowers. Some flowers are grown as a crop. Some flowers are grown to make perfume.

Sunflowers are grown as a crop. Sunflower seeds are used in animal feeds. The seeds are also crushed for their oil.

FLOWER FACTS

NUMBER OF KINDS OF FLOWERING PLANTS	more than 250 thousand
SIZE	up to 35 inches across
LIFE SPAN	flowering plants can live more than 100 years
ENEMIES	fungi, bacteria, some insects

brightly colored petals attract insects

male pollen grains on the anther join with female ovules of another flower

stamen

the parts of a flower

sepals part and open when the flower blooms

seedbox contains ovules which become seeds

Fly

see also: Insect, Mosquito

A fly is an insect. Flies live all over the world. Many flies carry germs. The germs can cause food poisoning and diseases, such as malaria and sleeping sickness.

Fly families

A large group of flies is called a swarm. A fly begins life as an egg. The egg hatches into a maggot. It looks like a small worm. The full-grown maggot changes into a pupa. Then it changes into an adult fly.

FLY FACTS

NUMBER OF KINDS	about 100 thousand
COLOR	usually black, gray, brown, or yellowish
LENGTH	less than an inch to 3 inches
STATUS	common
LIFE SPAN	up to 2 years
ENEMIES	spiders, birds, people, chemicals called insecticides

a housefly

thin, transparent wings can beat about 200 times a second

mouth like a sponge to soak up food

large eyes to see any movement

six legs used for walking; four legs used for standing

sticky pads on feet to walk upside down on ceilings

MEAT EATER

Some flies, such as mosquitoes, bite their prey. Then they suck up a drop of the prey's blood. Other flies, such as houseflies, spit on their food. Then they suck up the spit mixed with the food.

These blowfly maggots are feeding.

Folk Music

see also: Music, Musical Instrument

The first folk music was the music played or sung by people every day. People have always liked to sing together as they worked. They like to listen to other people sing. Folk musicians usually play guitars, fiddles, flutes, and harps.

Folk music today

Today there are professional folk musicians. Their job is to play instruments and sing. Many folk musicians give concerts. Other people play just for fun.

New folk music

Many old folk songs are still popular. Songs and tunes are handed down year after year from one musician to another. Folk music has also changed over the years. People play old songs on new instruments. People find new ways of playing old tunes. People are always writing new folk music, too.

These musicians are playing at an outdoor folk music concert.

Every country in the world has its own folk music. These musicians are from the Andes Mountains in South America.

CECIL SHARP (1859–1924)

Cecil Sharp, an Englishman, came to the United States in 1916. He was very interested in old folk songs and dances. He collected songs from the people living in the Appalachian Mountains. The people were singing songs that immigrants had brought with them from England 300 years before. People in England no longer knew the tunes to some of these songs. Now the songs are in Sharp's books and everyone can sing and play them.

Food Chain

see also: Animal, Plant

Animals eat to get energy. Some animals eat plants. Some animals eat other animals. A food chain shows how the energy passes from one creature to another.

From plants to animals

The first link in all food chains starts with plants. Animals that eat plants are called herbivores. That is the next link. Animals called carnivores eat other animals. They are the next link.

People and the food chain

Humans are in food chains, too. Most humans are omnivores. They eat both plants and animals.

Lions are carnivores. They are trying to catch and eat the plant-eating wildebeests.

This shows a food chain. The sun helps the rosebush to grow. The aphids eat the bush. The ladybug eats the aphids. The bird eats the ladybug. The cat eats the bird.

Forest

see also: Rain Forest, Tree, Wood

A forest is where many trees grow close together. Forests cover more than one third of all the land on Earth. Forests are homes for many kinds of birds, animals, and insects.

Types of forests

Forests in cold places mostly have coniferous trees. These are trees with needle leaves and cones. Fir and pine trees are coniferous. Forests in warm places mostly have deciduous trees. These are trees that have broad leaves that fall off once a year. Oak, elm, maple, and beech trees are deciduous trees. Tropical rain forests grow in places that are very hot and wet.

Trees have been cut down in large parts of the Amazon rain forest. The treeless land is not always good for growing crops.

People and forests

Forests are important to people. Trees make oxygen that people, animals, and plants need to breathe.

People are cutting down forests to open up land for farming. They are cutting down trees to sell the wood. They are doing this without planting new trees. In many countries, the forests are nearly gone.

Forests can create an environment where other plants can live. This eucalyptus forest in Australia is a good place for ferns to grow.

Fossil

see also: Dinosaur, Fuel

Fossils are formed from dead animals or plants. Looking at fossils tells us about animals and plants that lived a long time ago.

How fossils form

Plants leave behind leaves and stems. Animals leave behind bones or shells. What is left behind is covered with mud. When the mud turns to rock, the shape of the leaf, stem, bone, or shell stays in the rock. The shape in the rock is the fossil.

What fossils are found?

Some fossils are from creatures that are like animals that are still living today. Many fossils are from animals like dinosaurs that died out millions of years ago. Fossil bones tell us a lot about the size and shape of dinosaurs.

Coal is a fossil that people use as fuel. Coal is made from dead plants that have been squeezed hard and heated underground. Coal is called a fossil fuel.

DID YOU KNOW?

Chalk is a kind of fossil. It is made of the shells of tiny sea creatures that died millions of years ago.

This is a fossil of a fish. The fish lived 200 million years ago.

This scientist is working carefully on a rock with fossil remains. He can tell when the animals that made the fossils were alive.

Fox

see also: Coyote, Dog, Wolf

A fox is a mammal. It is a member of the dog family. Foxes are found almost everywhere north of the equator. The most common foxes are the red fox and the Arctic fox.

Fox families

A male is called a dog. A female is called a vixen. The babies are called cubs. A fox stays with its mate for its whole life. The vixen usually has four to five cubs at a time. Foxes dig a home called a den or earth. The dog fox usually hunts for food at night. The vixen looks after the cubs. Female cubs may stay with their parents for a year. Young males leave the den when they are about six months old.

FOX FACTS

NUMBER OF KINDS	21
COLOR	red, gray, or white
LENGTH	up to 32 inches
WEIGHT	about 22 lbs.
STATUS	common
LIFE SPAN	about 10 years
ENEMIES	Farmers sometimes kill foxes to protect chickens and other livestock.

long, full tail to keep warm while sleeping

sensitive nose to smell food and danger

strong legs for running

an American red fox

long muzzle for carrying food

sharp claws for digging

MEAT EATERS

A fox eats rabbits and small rodents. It also eats birds and eggs. Foxes will take chickens from farms. In autumn, foxes will eat soft fruit.

A female red fox looks after her three cubs in their den. These foxes live in the mountains of Montana.

France

see also: Europe

France is a country in western Europe. France has high mountains in the east and southwest. There are also big areas of lowland. The lowland has wide, winding rivers.

Living in France

Most people live in towns and cities. Most of the land is farmland. Farmers grow grain and grapes. Cheese is made from cows' and goats' milk. France is well-known for its food and its cooking. French cheeses, wine, bread, and mineral water are sold all over the world.

Cars, aircraft, clothes, and other goods are made in factories.

The main French festival is Bastille Day on July 14. This festival celebrates the French Revolution in 1789.

DID YOU KNOW?

The Eiffel Tower was built in 1889. Its designer was Alexandre Gustave Eiffel.

The Eiffel Tower is a famous landmark in Paris.

Europe

FACT FILE

PEOPLE	French
POPULATION	about 60 million
MAIN LANGUAGE	French
CAPITAL CITY	Paris
MONEY	Euro
HIGHEST MOUNTAIN	Mont Blanc—15,777 feet
LONGEST RIVER	Loire River—633 miles